30 Days to Inner Freedom: A Mindful Journey in Addiction Recovery

Kenneth Thomas

Published by Kenneth Thomas, 2024.

While every precaution has been taken in the preparation of this book, the publisher assumes no responsibility for errors or omissions, or for damages resulting from the use of the information contained herein.

30 DAYS TO INNER FREEDOM: A MINDFUL JOURNEY IN ADDICTION RECOVERY

First edition. November 10, 2024.

Copyright © 2024 Kenneth Thomas.

ISBN: 979-8227716415

Written by Kenneth Thomas.

Also by Kenneth Thomas

The Convergence of Minds series
The Digital Agora: A Philosophical Epic of AI and Humanity
Beyond the Agora: Fractured Realms

The Veil of Shadows Series
Shattered Dominion
The Fractured Path

Standalone
A Tail of Darkness To Light
The Mirror Within
Echoes of Ink and Heart
Purpose Over Power: The Visionary Path of Servant Leadership
The Questions That Shape Us: Finding Life's Wisdom-The Power of Inquiry
Where the Shadows Settle
30 Days to Inner Freedom: A Mindful Journey in Addiction Recovery

Dedication

Dedication
To those who find themselves standing at the edge, facing the struggles of addiction, and fighting battles unseen—this book is for you. Know that within you lies a strength greater than any obstacle, a light that, even if dimmed, is never truly extinguished.

This journey is not easy, but neither are you fragile. You are resilient, courageous, and capable of transformation. Every moment you choose to heal, every step forward, no matter how small, is a testament to the power within you. Recovery is not a straight path, but it is one worth walking, and you do not walk it alone. With each step, you honor yourself and the life waiting to unfold—a life of freedom, peace, and purpose.

May this book serve as a reminder of your strength and a companion through the challenges. Embrace each day with patience and know that you are worthy of healing, happiness, and the beauty of a new beginning. This journey is yours, and I dedicate this book to you, with respect and admiration for the courage it takes to rise and begin again.

30 Days to Inner Freedom: A Mindful Journey in Addiction Recovery

Introduction

Welcome to a journey of healing, growth, and self-discovery. If you're here, reading these words, it means you've already taken one of the most courageous steps a person can take: the decision to choose recovery. This choice to pursue inner freedom and break free from old cycles is not easy, but it's powerful. Acknowledging the need for change requires immense strength, honesty, and a deep commitment to yourself - and that's exactly what this journey will help you build upon, day by day.

30 Days to Inner Freedom is not a quick fix or a magic cure. It's a compassionate guide designed to be your steady companion, supporting you through the complex and often winding path of recovery. Over the next 30 days, you'll find insights, reflections, and practices to help you rediscover your inner strength, cultivate self-compassion, and renew your sense of purpose.

Recovery is often seen as a battle, something to be conquered. But here, we'll approach it as a mindful journey - one that leads you inward, toward greater understanding, acceptance, and resilience. It's not just about breaking free from addiction; it's about rebuilding your life from a place of self-respect, clarity, and inner peace. Each day, you'll work on strengthening these foundations through mindfulness, affirmations, and moments of gratitude, creating habits and mindsets that will guide you well beyond these 30 days.

What You'll Find in This Guide

Each day in this guide has been crafted with three elements: Stoic wisdom, daily affirmations, and gratitude meditation. Together, these practices offer both ancient and modern tools to help you navigate the ups and downs of recovery with calm, resilience, and purpose. Let's explore how each of these elements will support your journey.

Stoic Wisdom: Stoicism, a philosophy embraced by ancient thinkers like Marcus Aurelius and Seneca, offers timeless wisdom for navigating life's challenges with grace, resilience, and clarity. Each day begins with a quote from Stoic philosophy - a reminder of the strength that comes from self-discipline, self-reflection, and acceptance. These quotes provide encouragement and guidance, inviting you to approach each day's challenges with the perspective that you are capable, that you have a choice, and that you can find peace even in difficult moments.

Daily Affirmations: Affirmations are powerful tools for building self-worth, reframing negative thoughts, and reinforcing the beliefs that guide you. The affirmations you'll find in this guide have been carefully crafted with principles from neuro-linguistic programming (NLP) to help reshape thought patterns, anchor you in positive self-identity, and keep you focused on recovery. By repeating these affirmations, you'll begin to internalize a new self-image, one rooted in courage, resilience, and hope. Some of these affirmations may feel challenging, especially if you've struggled with self-doubt or self-worth. That's okay. These words are meant to gently guide you toward seeing the person you are becoming.

Gratitude Meditation: Gratitude is one of the simplest yet most transformative practices for recovery. Each day, we'll end with a gratitude meditation that centers on the present moment, helping you shift from the struggles of the past to the possibilities of today. Gratitude allows you to see the good that exists within and around you, even in small ways. Practicing gratitude will help you reframe your experience, reinforcing the idea that each moment - even the challenging ones - has value. Over time, gratitude will help you cultivate a resilient, hopeful mindset, one that can carry you forward even on difficult days.

How to Use This Book

This journey is yours, and it's meant to unfold at a pace that feels right for you. Each day's exercises are designed to take about 15 to

20 minutes, but feel free to move through them at your own rhythm. Some days may feel lighter and easier, while others may require more emotional energy. Both are normal and welcome on this path. If you ever feel overwhelmed, remember that you can take a pause. You're encouraged to revisit any reflection, affirmation, or meditation that resonates with you, returning to them as often as you need. This guide is a steady support - not a rigid program - so use it as a resource to find the peace, strength, and clarity you seek.

Your Path to Inner Freedom

This journey to inner freedom is uniquely yours. Recovery is deeply personal, and the challenges, setbacks, and victories you encounter are part of what makes it meaningful. You may come across moments of doubt or temptation; you may face difficult emotions you've held onto for a long time. But remember: you're not here to be perfect. You're here to create a life built on resilience, self-respect, and true freedom - free from the burdens of addiction and free to live as the person you truly are.

Over the next 30 days, let this book be a safe place where you can explore, grow, and rebuild. Give yourself the grace to grow slowly, to make mistakes, and to find joy in small victories. Each day, with each mindful breath, each affirmation, and each moment of gratitude, you're laying the foundation for a life defined not by the past but by your courage, resilience, and dedication to becoming your best self.

Through this mindful journey, you are not only breaking free from addiction - you're rediscovering what it means to be free within. Inner freedom means living from a place of self-awareness, peace, and purpose. It's about aligning with your values, honoring your journey, and knowing that you are enough exactly as you are. So let's begin, one step at a time, and see where this journey to inner freedom leads.

Chapter 1

Day 1: Embracing the First Step
Stoic Quote of the Day
"The first step: Don't be anxious. Nature controls it all. And before long you'll be no one, nowhere, like Hadrian, like Augustus. The second step: Concentrate on what you have to do. Fix your eyes on it. Remind yourself that your task is to be a good human being; remind yourself what nature demands of people."
- Marcus Aurelius
Reflection: Marcus Aurelius reminds us that our first step is to release anxiety about the past and future and focus on what is directly in front of us. Recovery is not about conquering everything at once; it's about taking each day, each moment, as it comes. Right now, your task is simply to show up for yourself, to commit to this journey, and to recognize that each small step will lead you forward. Today, let go of the need to have all the answers and focus on the courage it took just to begin.
5 Affirmations for Day 1
"I honor the courage it took to begin this journey, knowing I am worthy of this change."
"I am present with each step, trusting the process and allowing myself to grow."
I am grateful for the positive change in my life, no matter how small the step."
"Each breath brings me closer to the peace I am seeking."
"Today, I am fully committed to showing up for myself, one moment at a time."
Gratitude Meditation: Honoring the First Step

Begin with Gentle Awareness: Sit comfortably in a quiet place, allowing yourself to settle into a peaceful posture. Close your eyes and take a few deep, calming breaths, inhaling through the nose and exhaling gently through the mouth. Feel the air filling your lungs, and as you exhale, release any tension or anxiety about the journey ahead.

Recognize Your Inner Strength: As you continue breathing, bring your awareness to the strength it took to reach this moment. Recognize the courage within you that has led you to commit to this journey. In your mind, silently say, "Thank you," honoring this powerful decision and the strength it reflects.

Express Gratitude for a Fresh Start: Now, gently shift your focus to the opportunity that today brings. You have a new beginning - a chance to move forward with compassion and purpose. Feel gratitude for the ability to create positive change, no matter where you're starting. Picture this gratitude as a soft, warm light in your chest, expanding with each breath.

Focus on Three Things You're Grateful For:

First, express gratitude for your own resilience - the part of you that refuses to give up and seeks growth and healing.

Second, give thanks for the support in your life, whether it's from loved ones, a friend, or even this guide.

Third, appreciate the small victories of today - the quiet moments, the breath you're taking right now, or even this step toward self-discovery and freedom.

Visualize Growth: Finally, imagine that today's choice to begin is like planting a seed. See it in your mind's eye - a small, strong seed full of potential, ready to grow with care, patience, and time. This seed is your recovery journey. Picture it being nourished with each mindful breath, each compassionate thought, each step forward.

End with Gratitude: Take a final deep breath, feeling this seed of growth within you. When you're ready, bring a gentle smile to your face, honoring yourself for showing up. Open your eyes softly, carrying a sense of gratitude and self-compassion with you as you move through your day.

Reflection for Today

In a journal or a quiet space, take a few minutes to reflect on today's experience. Ask yourself:

What does taking this first step mean to me?

How do I feel about the journey I am beginning?

What qualities within myself do I want to nurture as I move forward?

Remember, today is about celebrating the decision to begin, honoring the strength it took to choose recovery, and trusting in the small, steady steps that will carry you forward. Each day is a new opportunity to build upon this foundation. Welcome to your journey to inner freedom.

Chapter 2

Day 2: Understanding Triggers and Patterns

Stoic Quote of the Day

"If you are pained by external things, it is not they that disturb you, but your own judgment of them. And it is in your power to wipe out that judgment now."

- Marcus Aurelius

Reflection: Marcus Aurelius reminds us that often, it's not the situation itself that holds power over us, but our reactions to it. This insight is especially powerful in recovery. The things that trigger cravings or stress may feel overwhelming, yet they're often just cues that reveal underlying beliefs, habits, or responses. Today, focus on understanding the triggers and patterns that affect you without judging yourself. Recognizing these patterns can be a powerful step toward freeing yourself from their hold.

5 Affirmations for Day 2

"I have the power to observe my triggers and respond with compassion and clarity."

"I am patient with myself as I uncover the roots of my behaviors and emotions."

"I recognize that my triggers are temporary and do not define me."

"Each trigger I understand brings me closer to freedom and resilience."

"I choose how I respond, and today I choose awareness, calm, and courage."

Gratitude Meditation: Acknowledging the Journey

Settle into Stillness: Find a comfortable position, sitting upright with your hands resting gently on your knees or in your lap. Close your eyes, and take three deep, slow breaths, releasing any tension you feel as you exhale.

Bring Awareness to the Body: Notice the sensations in your body as you sit quietly, feeling the weight of your body supported by the ground or chair. As you breathe, become aware of any areas of tightness or stress, and with each breath, allow those areas to soften.

Reflect on Three Things You're Grateful For:

First, express gratitude for your awareness, the ability to notice patterns in your thoughts and actions. Recognize that self-awareness is a powerful step toward positive change.

Second, acknowledge any supportive resources or people in your life who encourage your growth and healing. Feel gratitude for their presence, guidance, or even just the feeling that you're not alone.

Third, appreciate the strength within yourself - the part of you that is open to understanding and working through challenges. Thank yourself for your willingness to do this important work.

Visualize Letting Go of Judgment: Now, bring to mind one trigger or challenge you've faced in the past. See it as a small object, something you can observe in your mind's eye without judgment. Allow it to float in front of you like a leaf on water. Notice it, breathe, and let it drift away as you release any need to control it. Observe without attachment, knowing that this is simply a part of the journey.

End with Appreciation: As you take a final deep breath, bring your attention back to the present. Acknowledge the growth that comes from observing your thoughts, emotions, and triggers with patience and kindness. When you're ready, open your eyes, feeling grateful for the progress you've made today.

Reflection for Today

In your journal or in a quiet space, take a few minutes to reflect on today's exploration. Consider these prompts:

What triggers have I noticed in my life that influence my emotions or cravings?

How do I typically react to these triggers, and how might I choose to respond differently?

What small actions can I take to observe these triggers without judgment?

Today, remember that awareness is power. By recognizing your patterns and triggers, you're taking the first steps toward reclaiming your response. Each day brings you closer to inner freedom through patience, understanding, and choice. You're building resilience, one mindful observation at a time.

Chapter 3

Day 3: Cultivating Self-Compassion
Stoic Quote of the Day
"What progress, you ask, have I made? I have begun to be a friend to myself."
- Hecato of Rhodes
Reflection: Today's quote reminds us of the value of being kind and gentle with ourselves. Recovery can stir up feelings of regret, shame, or self-criticism, but true healing requires that we treat ourselves with compassion. Being a friend to yourself means recognizing your worth beyond any mistakes, embracing your strengths, and forgiving yourself as you grow. Today, focus on nurturing self-compassion and letting go of harsh judgments. Treat yourself with the same kindness you would offer to someone you love.
5 Affirmations for Day 3
"I am worthy of kindness, patience, and understanding from myself."
"I choose to be gentle with myself as I walk this path of recovery."
"I am learning, growing, and healing, and I allow myself the grace to do so."
"I forgive myself for past mistakes, understanding they do not define me."
"Today, I am my own ally, supporting my growth with compassion."
Gratitude Meditation: Honoring Yourself with Compassion
Find a Comfortable Position: Sit in a quiet place, allowing yourself to relax. Rest your hands gently on your lap, close your eyes, and take a few deep breaths, focusing on the rise and fall of your chest. Let each exhale release tension from your body.

Reflect on Your Strengths: Bring to mind one quality you appreciate about yourself - a strength, talent, or kind gesture. It could be something as simple as your ability to listen or your determination to grow. Allow yourself to feel gratitude for this quality, recognizing that it is a unique part of who you are.

Acknowledge Your Resilience: Now, focus on the resilience that has brought you to this point. Recovery requires bravery, courage, and endurance. Thank yourself for the resilience within you, the part of you that is committed to healing, even when it's challenging.

Gratitude for Self-Compassion:

First, give thanks for your capacity to care for yourself, no matter how difficult it feels. Appreciate the moments of kindness and patience you show yourself, big or small.

Second, recognize that self-compassion is a practice - one that you're willing to nurture and grow. Feel gratitude for the openness within you to cultivate this quality.

Third, acknowledge that you are enough, right here, right now. Allow yourself to let go of any need to be perfect and simply be present with who you are today.

Visualize Self-Compassion as a Warm Light: Imagine a warm, golden light in the center of your chest, representing compassion. With each breath, let this light expand, filling your chest, your entire body, and finally surrounding you like a soft, comforting glow. This light is your self-compassion, radiating kindness and warmth. Know that this compassion is always within you, ready to support and guide you.

End with Appreciation: Take a final deep breath, bringing your awareness back to the room around you. When you're ready, open your eyes with a gentle smile, feeling gratitude for the strength and self-compassion you're cultivating.

Reflection for Today

In your journal or during a quiet moment, consider these reflection prompts:

What is one thing I appreciate about myself today?
How can I be more compassionate with myself as I continue this journey?
How would my life feel different if I consistently treated myself as a friend?

Today, remember that compassion isn't just something we give to others; it's a gift we give to ourselves. Allow yourself the grace to be kind, patient, and forgiving. Embrace the progress you're making, knowing that each act of self-compassion is a step closer to inner peace and freedom.

Chapter 4

Day 4: Building a Support System

Stoic Quote of the Day

"We are like branches on a tree, all growing in different directions yet stemming from the same source."

- Seneca

Reflection: Seneca reminds us of the importance of connection. We all walk unique paths, but our lives are interwoven, and we are supported by others even when we feel alone. In recovery, a support system can be one of your greatest sources of strength. Today, reflect on the people who uplift you and the resources that help you stay grounded. Remember that seeking support isn't a sign of weakness - it's a courageous act of self-care. Building and embracing a network of support can make this journey feel more manageable, purposeful, and meaningful.

5 Affirmations for Day 4

"I am open to receiving support from those who genuinely care for my well-being."

"I am deserving of a community that uplifts and encourages me."

"I am not alone on this journey, and I welcome the strength that others provide."

"I am grateful for the people who support my growth and healing."

"Today, I will reach out to those who empower and inspire me."

Gratitude Meditation: Recognizing Your Support System

Settle into a Comfortable Position: Find a quiet place to sit, either on the floor or in a chair. Close your eyes, relax your shoulders, and take a few deep breaths. With each exhale, release any tension you feel, allowing yourself to settle into a state of calm.

Begin with Self-Gratitude: Start by acknowledging your own courage and determination to seek support. Recognize that choosing to build a support system is a powerful step in your recovery, and thank yourself for being open to this choice.

Bring to Mind Three People or Sources of Support:

First, think of one person who has been a consistent source of encouragement in your life, someone who genuinely cares for your well-being. Take a moment to feel gratitude for their presence and support, recognizing the comfort they bring.

Second, focus on someone who has inspired you in some way. This could be a friend, family member, mentor, or even an inspiring figure you admire from afar. Feel gratitude for the ways this person motivates you to grow and reminds you of your own potential.

Third, acknowledge a community or group (like a support group, online community, or close-knit circle of friends) that provides you with strength, understanding, and solidarity. Thank them for the sense of belonging they offer, appreciating the comfort and support of a shared journey.

Visualize a Web of Connection: Now, visualize yourself at the center of a web, with threads connecting you to each person or source of support. Imagine that each connection is strong and supportive, radiating warmth and encouragement. Know that even when you feel alone, this network is here to uplift and empower you.

End with a Breath of Gratitude: Take a final deep breath, and as you exhale, feel a sense of gratitude for each connection that enriches your life. Open your eyes slowly, carrying this feeling of support and connection with you into the day ahead.

Reflection for Today

In a journal or during a quiet moment, reflect on these prompts:

Who are three people I can reach out to for support, encouragement, or inspiration?

How does it feel to lean on others during this journey?

What specific steps can I take to strengthen my support system today? Today, let go of any hesitation about seeking support and allow yourself to embrace connection. Building a support system is not only an act of self-care, but it's also a reminder that you don't have to navigate recovery alone. Each connection you nurture brings you closer to a life filled with compassion, resilience, and inner peace.

Chapter 5

Day 5: Embracing Resilience in the Face of Setbacks

Stoic Quote of the Day

"The greater the difficulty, the more glory in surmounting it. Skillful pilots gain their reputation from storms and tempests."

- Epictetus

Reflection: Epictetus reminds us that challenges and setbacks are part of every journey. They don't define our worth or our potential; instead, they offer us the opportunity to grow stronger and more resilient. Recovery isn't about achieving perfection; it's about learning to navigate setbacks with patience and compassion. Today, allow yourself to see resilience as a skill that you can nurture. Each setback is not a failure but a step on the path to a deeper, lasting freedom.

5 Affirmations for Day 5

"I am resilient, capable of facing setbacks with grace and strength."

"I view setbacks as opportunities to learn and grow on my journey."

"I am patient with myself as I grow, allowing room for mistakes and learning."

"I am committed to my progress, no matter how winding the path may be."

"Each challenge I face strengthens my resolve and brings me closer to freedom."

Gratitude Meditation: Cultivating Strength and Resilience

Begin in Stillness: Find a quiet place to sit comfortably. Close your eyes, take a deep breath in through your nose, and slowly exhale through your mouth. With each breath, release any tension, settling into a calm and centered state.

Reflect on Past Resilience: Bring to mind a challenge you've faced in the past, something difficult that you managed to overcome. It doesn't have to be directly related to recovery; it could be anything that required courage or resilience. Take a moment to feel gratitude for the strength you showed during that time, knowing that same strength is within you today.

Acknowledge Your Commitment to Growth: Shift your focus to your current journey in recovery. Thank yourself for the commitment you've shown, the patience you've cultivated, and the growth you're pursuing. Recognize that, like any journey worth taking, recovery includes obstacles that make the progress even more meaningful.

Gratitude for Today's Challenges:

First, express gratitude for the resilience you are developing - the strength that grows each time you face a setback or challenge.

Second, acknowledge the opportunity to learn from mistakes or difficult moments. Appreciate that each experience offers valuable lessons that bring you closer to a deeper understanding of yourself.

Third, thank yourself for being patient and compassionate with your journey, recognizing that each small act of kindness toward yourself is a testament to your inner strength.

Visualize Resilience as a Flame Within You: Picture a small, steady flame at the center of your chest. This flame represents your resilience. See it growing stronger and brighter with each breath, illuminating your entire being with warmth and light. Know that this flame is always with you, ready to guide you through both smooth and stormy days.

End with a Breath of Gratitude: Take a final deep breath, filling yourself with gratitude for your resilience and determination. As you exhale, feel a sense of peace and readiness to face whatever comes your way today. When you're ready, gently open your eyes, carrying this feeling of resilience with you.

Reflection for Today

In your journal or during a quiet moment, reflect on the following prompts:
What are some challenges I have overcome in the past, and what did I learn from them?
How do I feel about setbacks on my journey? How might I reframe them as opportunities for growth?
What are some small actions I can take to strengthen my resilience each day?
Today, remember that resilience isn't a trait you either have or lack - it's a skill you build with each experience. Embrace setbacks as part of the journey, and know that each one brings you closer to true freedom, strength, and inner peace. You have the power to turn every challenge into an opportunity to grow stronger, wiser, and more compassionate toward yourself.

Chapter 6

Day 6: Practicing Mindful Awareness of Cravings

Stoic Quote of the Day

"Freedom is the only worthy goal in life. It is won by disregarding things that lie beyond our control."

- Epictetus

Reflection: Epictetus reminds us that freedom comes from focusing on what we can control. In recovery, cravings are a natural part of the journey. While we may not be able to stop them from arising, we have the power to choose how we respond to them. Today, focus on observing cravings without judgment, recognizing them as temporary experiences rather than commands you have to obey. Each craving offers you the opportunity to strengthen your awareness and build resilience.

5 Affirmations for Day 6

"I am capable of observing my cravings without judgment or fear.".

"Cravings are temporary, and I am in control of my response to them."

"I trust my strength and patience to guide me through challenging moments."

"I am separate from my cravings; they do not define or control me."

"With each craving I overcome, I grow stronger and closer to my inner freedom."

Gratitude Meditation: Finding Peace Amidst Cravings

Begin by Calming the Breath: Sit comfortably, with your back straight and your hands resting in your lap. Close your eyes, take a deep breath in through the nose, and exhale slowly through the mouth. Focus on each breath, letting yourself sink into calmness and presence.

Acknowledge the Presence of Cravings: As you sit quietly, bring to mind the cravings or urges you may experience. Instead of resisting or fighting them, simply acknowledge them. See them as visitors passing through - a natural part of your journey. Remind yourself that cravings are temporary and do not define your strength or your progress.

Reflect on Three Things You're Grateful For:

First, express gratitude for your awareness - the ability to observe your cravings without reacting impulsively. Acknowledge that awareness is the first step to gaining freedom from unwanted habits.

Second, thank yourself for the patience and control you are building by learning to sit with discomfort. Each time you observe a craving without acting, you strengthen your inner resilience.

Third, appreciate the calm and peace within you, even if it feels small right now. Know that this inner peace grows stronger each time you choose awareness over reaction.

Visualize Cravings as Passing Clouds: Imagine that each craving or urge is like a cloud drifting across the sky. Watch it come and go, floating past you without affecting your sense of calm. Remind yourself that cravings are just thoughts - they appear, but they don't need to control you. Feel gratitude for the ability to observe without attachment.

End with a Breath of Gratitude: Take a final deep breath, feeling grounded and thankful for your strength, awareness, and growing resilience. When you're ready, open your eyes, carrying this calm and mindful presence into the rest of your day.

Reflection for Today

In a journal or during a quiet moment, reflect on these prompts:

How do I typically respond to cravings, and what have I learned from observing them?

What are some ways I can remind myself that cravings are temporary?

How do I feel after observing cravings rather than acting on them?

Today, practice treating your cravings as passing experiences rather than obstacles or failures. By observing them calmly, you're taking control of your journey and building a new relationship with your thoughts. Each time you overcome a craving, you move closer to inner freedom, strengthening your ability to choose a path of peace, patience, and strength.

Chapter 7

Day 7: Developing Emotional Awareness
Stoic Quote of the Day
"You have power over your mind - not outside events. Realize this, and you will find strength."
- Marcus Aurelius
Reflection: Marcus Aurelius teaches us that true power lies in how we handle our own mind and emotions. In recovery, it's essential to become aware of your emotional landscape - to notice and name your feelings without letting them control you. Today, focus on observing your emotions as they arise, understanding them without judgment. The goal isn't to suppress or ignore feelings but to acknowledge them, giving yourself space to respond calmly and constructively. By developing emotional awareness, you create the foundation for a balanced, resilient mind.
5 Affirmations for Day 7
"I am open to understanding my emotions with patience and kindness."
"My feelings are valid, and I allow myself to experience them fully."
"I am not defined by my emotions; they are simply experiences that come and go."
"I am calm and resilient, even when I experience intense emotions."
"With each emotion I understand, I grow stronger and more self-aware."
Gratitude Meditation: Embracing Emotional Awareness
Find Your Center: Sit comfortably, with your back straight and hands resting on your lap. Close your eyes and take three deep breaths, inhaling slowly through your nose and exhaling through your mouth.

Let each breath bring you into a calm, present state, releasing any tension.

Welcome Your Emotional Landscape: Take a moment to notice any emotions you may be experiencing right now. You don't need to analyze or judge them - just observe. Whether you're feeling calm, anxious, hopeful, or frustrated, acknowledge each emotion as it arises, giving it space without attachment.

Reflect on Three Things You're Grateful For:

First, express gratitude for your ability to feel and experience emotions - this is part of being fully alive. Recognize that emotions, both pleasant and challenging, are part of your journey and offer valuable insights.

Second, give thanks for the awareness you are cultivating, which allows you to understand and navigate your emotional responses. Appreciate that this awareness is helping you make choices from a place of understanding rather than reaction.

Third, appreciate the strength within you to hold space for each emotion, knowing that you are not defined by any single feeling. This strength is what empowers you to observe and grow through each experience.

Visualize Emotions as Waves on the Ocean: Picture each emotion as a gentle wave on the ocean, rising and falling naturally. Some waves are calm and small, while others are larger and more intense. Imagine yourself as the observer, sitting on the shore and watching these waves. Notice that, like waves, emotions rise, peak, and eventually fade away. Feel gratitude for the peace of mind that comes from being able to observe without being pulled under.

End with a Breath of Gratitude: Take a final deep breath, feeling a sense of appreciation for your growing emotional awareness. Recognize that each emotion you observe brings you closer to self-understanding and inner balance. When you're ready, gently open your eyes, carrying this sense of calm and awareness with you into the rest of your day.

Reflection for Today

In a journal or during a quiet moment, consider these reflection prompts:
What emotions did I notice today, and how did I respond to them?
How does observing my emotions without reacting to them change my experience?
What are some ways I can continue to develop emotional awareness as I move forward?
Today, remember that emotions are not obstacles but valuable signals guiding you toward greater self-understanding. By observing them without judgment, you're building resilience, emotional balance, and clarity. Each time you choose awareness over reaction, you strengthen your foundation of inner peace and freedom.

Chapter 8

Day 8: Replacing Old Habits with Positive Alternatives
Stoic Quote of the Day
"First say to yourself what you would be; and then do what you have to do."
- Epictetus
Reflection: Epictetus encourages us to envision who we want to become and align our actions with that vision. Recovery is not only about breaking old habits but also about forming new ones that support the life you want to live. Today, focus on identifying old habits that no longer serve you and explore positive alternatives. Each time you choose a new, healthy action, you're building a stronger foundation for lasting change and inner freedom.
5 Affirmations for Day 8
"I am capable of transforming my habits to support my growth and well-being."
"Every small choice I make today contributes to my journey of healing and freedom."
"I am creating a life that reflects my values, strengths, and goals."
"I let go of habits that no longer serve me and embrace ones that support my highest self."
"I am patient with myself as I build new habits, knowing that each step brings progress."
Gratitude Meditation: Welcoming Positive Change
Begin with Centered Breathing: Sit comfortably, close your eyes, and take three deep breaths. As you inhale, imagine drawing in calm and clarity. As you exhale, release any tension, letting go of old patterns or habits that may be weighing you down.

Bring to Mind One Habit You Want to Replace: Think about one habit you wish to change. Acknowledge it without judgment, simply recognizing it as something that may have served you in the past but is no longer aligned with who you want to become.

Reflect on Three Positive Alternatives You're Grateful For:
First, express gratitude for the awareness and strength that have allowed you to recognize the need for change. Acknowledge that self-awareness is the first step toward transformation.

Second, appreciate the positive alternatives available to you - new habits or actions that support your recovery and well-being. This could be choosing exercise, a hobby, or a meaningful activity in place of an old habit.

Third, give thanks for the progress you've made so far and for the patience you're cultivating in the process. Each step, no matter how small, is part of the journey toward a healthier, more fulfilling life.

Visualize Embracing New Habits as Small Acts of Self-Love: Picture each new, positive habit as a gentle act of self-love. See yourself choosing these new actions, and imagine them becoming easier and more natural over time. Feel gratitude for the strength within you to make these choices, recognizing that each one is a gift you give to yourself.

End with a Breath of Appreciation: Take a final deep breath, filling yourself with a sense of gratitude for your commitment to positive change. When you're ready, gently open your eyes, carrying this feeling of appreciation and resolve with you.

Reflection for Today
In a journal or during a quiet moment, reflect on these prompts:
What old habit do I want to let go of, and what positive alternative can I embrace instead?
How does this new habit align with my vision of the person I want to become?

What small, consistent actions can I take to integrate this positive habit into my daily life?

Today, remember that lasting change happens through small, intentional choices. By replacing old habits with actions that reflect your true values, you are not only reshaping your day-to-day life but also building the foundation for a healthier, freer, and more fulfilling future.

Chapter 9

Day 9: Cultivating Patience with the Process
Stoic Quote of the Day
"No great thing is created suddenly, any more than a bunch of grapes or a fig. If you tell me that you desire a fig, I answer you that there must be time. Let it first blossom, then bear fruit, then ripen."
- Epictetus
Reflection: Epictetus reminds us that meaningful change takes time. Recovery is a journey that unfolds gradually, requiring patience and trust in the process. It's natural to want quick results, but true growth comes from small, steady steps. Today, focus on practicing patience with yourself. Recognize that each moment, each action, and each decision you make is part of a larger picture. Allow yourself the time to blossom, grow, and transform at your own pace.
5 Affirmations for Day 9
"I am patient with myself and my progress, trusting that each step brings me closer to my goals."
"I honor the pace of my journey and give myself time to heal fully."
"I am committed to steady growth, knowing that lasting change takes time."
"Each day, I grow stronger and more resilient, no matter how small the progress."
"I am grateful for each small step, knowing they add up to profound transformation."
Gratitude Meditation: Embracing Patience in Your Journey
Begin by Finding Stillness: Sit comfortably, with your eyes closed and hands resting on your lap. Take a few deep breaths, inhaling deeply and

exhaling slowly. As you breathe, allow yourself to settle into a state of calm, letting go of any urgency or impatience.

Acknowledge Your Progress: Reflect on the progress you've made, no matter how small. Give yourself credit for showing up each day, for the steps you've taken, and for the commitment you've shown. Feel gratitude for every bit of growth, knowing that these small steps are building something meaningful.

Reflect on Three Things You're Grateful For:

First, express gratitude for the patience you are learning to cultivate, understanding that change is a process that takes time.

Second, thank yourself for the strength to stay committed, even on the days when progress feels slow or challenging.

Third, appreciate the moments of growth, big or small, that remind you that you are capable of transformation. Each bit of progress, no matter how minor it may seem, is a sign of your resilience.

Visualize Your Journey as a Growing Tree: Imagine your journey as a tree that grows taller and stronger each day. Picture its roots reaching deep into the earth, stable and secure, while its branches stretch toward the sky. Know that, like this tree, your growth is gradual but constant, and each day's progress adds strength and resilience to your foundation.

End with a Breath of Appreciation: Take a final deep breath, feeling a sense of gratitude for the journey you're on. Recognize that patience with yourself is a powerful gift. When you're ready, open your eyes, carrying a sense of peace and acceptance with you as you move forward in your day.

Reflection for Today

In a journal or during a quiet moment, reflect on these prompts:

What are some small signs of progress I've noticed in my recovery so far?

How can I remind myself to be patient on days when growth feels slow?

What does it mean to me to trust the process and allow myself time to heal?

Today, remember that transformation is a gradual journey. Each small step, each moment of patience, and each decision to keep moving forward contributes to your growth. Embrace the process, knowing that you are exactly where you need to be, and trust that each day's progress brings you closer to inner freedom and lasting change.

Chapter 10

Day 10: Practicing Self-Forgiveness
Stoic Quote of the Day
"To bear trials with a calm mind robs misfortune of its strength and burden."
- Seneca
Reflection: Seneca teaches us that carrying burdens with a calm and understanding mind can transform our experience of hardship. Recovery often brings up feelings of guilt, regret, or shame - emotions tied to past actions and choices. Today, focus on releasing these burdens through the practice of self-forgiveness. Forgiving yourself doesn't mean condoning past actions; it means releasing their hold on you so you can move forward with peace. Allow yourself the grace to accept your past, learn from it, and step forward with compassion.
5 Affirmations for Day 10
"I am willing to forgive myself and release the weight of the past."
NLP Focus: Emphasizes willingness and release, creating mental space for self-compassion.
"I choose to see myself with compassion, accepting both my strengths and imperfections."
"I learn from my past and use its lessons to grow wiser and stronger."
"I am free from the burden of guilt; I embrace healing and peace."
"Today, I give myself permission to move forward with a light heart and a clear mind."
Gratitude Meditation: Embracing Self-Forgiveness
Begin with Gentle Breathing: Find a quiet place to sit comfortably. Close your eyes, place your hands on your lap, and take three slow, deep

breaths. With each exhale, imagine releasing any tension or heaviness in your body, allowing yourself to settle into a calm and accepting state.
Bring to Mind a Moment of Regret: Think about a moment from your past that still weighs on you, a situation or choice that brings up feelings of guilt or regret. Acknowledge it without judgment, recognizing that this moment is part of your journey, one that helped shape who you are today.
Reflect on Three Things You're Grateful For:
First, express gratitude for your willingness to forgive - the choice you're making to release the past and embrace peace.
Second, thank yourself for the lessons you've learned from past experiences, appreciating the wisdom gained through challenges.
Third, appreciate your growth and commitment to change, recognizing that you are moving forward with each day.
Visualize Self-Forgiveness as a Gentle Light: Imagine a soft, warm light filling your chest, radiating kindness and compassion. This light represents forgiveness, soothing any lingering feelings of guilt or regret. With each breath, let this light grow brighter, filling you with acceptance and peace. Visualize it washing over any painful memories, softening them until they no longer feel like burdens.
End with a Breath of Release: Take a final deep breath, feeling a sense of release and gratitude for the peace you are cultivating. Know that each moment of self-forgiveness brings you closer to freedom and self-compassion. When you're ready, open your eyes, carrying a sense of lightness and renewal into the day.
Reflection for Today
In your journal or during a quiet moment, reflect on these prompts:
What past actions or decisions am I ready to forgive myself for?
How does it feel to let go of guilt and embrace self-compassion?
What steps can I take to remind myself that I am worthy of forgiveness and growth?

Today, remember that self-forgiveness is not about erasing the past; it's about releasing its grip on your present. By letting go of guilt and embracing compassion, you free yourself to live more fully, with a heart that is open to healing, peace, and transformation. Each moment of forgiveness is a step toward inner freedom.

Chapter 11

Day 11: Building Self-Trust
Stoic Quote of the Day
"If you are distressed by anything external, the pain is not due to the thing itself, but to your estimate of it; and this you have the power to revoke at any moment."
- Marcus Aurelius
Reflection: Marcus Aurelius teaches us that our perception of events holds more power over us than the events themselves. In recovery, self-trust can feel fragile, especially if past choices led to setbacks or regret. Today, focus on rebuilding trust with yourself. Trust isn't about never making mistakes; it's about believing in your capacity to grow, learn, and make choices that reflect your true values. Each step forward, no matter how small, is a testament to your strength and commitment.
5 Affirmations for Day 11
"I am rebuilding trust with myself, one choice at a time."
NLP Focus: Emphasizes gradual progress, building confidence in small, intentional steps.
"I honor my intentions and follow through on what is best for my well-being."
"I am capable of making decisions that support my growth and freedom."
"With each promise I keep to myself, I strengthen my trust and resilience."
"I trust myself to create a life that reflects my values, strengths, and goals."
Gratitude Meditation: Nurturing Self-Trust

Begin with Deep Breathing: Sit comfortably, close your eyes, and take a few slow, deep breaths. With each inhale, imagine drawing in calm and confidence; with each exhale, release any doubts or fears, settling into a place of self-assurance.

Acknowledge Past Moments of Self-Trust: Reflect on a time in your life when you followed through on something important, when you kept a promise to yourself or achieved a goal. Recognize that this experience, no matter how small, shows your capacity for integrity and commitment. Feel gratitude for these moments, as they are the foundation of self-trust.

Reflect on Three Things You're Grateful For:

First, express gratitude for your courage to rebuild trust with yourself, appreciating the strength it takes to keep showing up for your growth.

Second, thank yourself for the resilience you've shown in recovery, each day reinforcing your ability to make choices that honor your well-being.

Third, appreciate the journey of self-discovery you're on, as each day brings you closer to a life that aligns with your true self and values.

Visualize Self-Trust as a Growing Tree Within You: Imagine self-trust as a small tree rooted in your heart. Each promise you keep, each compassionate choice, and each positive action adds strength to this tree, helping it grow. Picture its branches reaching higher with each breath, symbolizing the trust you are cultivating within yourself.

End with a Breath of Assurance: Take a final deep breath, filling yourself with a sense of self-assurance and calm. Feel gratitude for the self-trust you're building, knowing that with each day, you're becoming more aligned with your authentic self. When you're ready, gently open your eyes, carrying this renewed sense of trust into the day ahead.

Reflection for Today

In your journal or during a quiet moment, reflect on these prompts:

What actions or promises can I keep to strengthen my trust in myself?

How does it feel to believe in my capacity to make positive choices?

What can I do today to honor my commitment to my recovery journey? Today, remember that self-trust is built through consistent, compassionate choices. Each action you take to honor yourself and your growth reinforces a foundation of inner confidence and resilience. With each promise you keep, you're building a life rooted in integrity, strength, and freedom. Trust yourself to navigate this journey - you are stronger and more capable than you realize.

Chapter 12

Day 12: Embracing Self-Worth
Stoic Quote of the Day
"Never esteem anything as of advantage to you that will make you break your word or lose your self-respect."
- Marcus Aurelius
Reflection: Marcus Aurelius reminds us that our self-respect and integrity are far more valuable than anything gained at their expense. Recovery is a journey of rediscovering and embracing your inherent worth - learning that you are valuable not because of what you achieve but simply because of who you are. Today, focus on cultivating a deep sense of self-worth, knowing that you deserve love, respect, and kindness from yourself and others. By honoring your worth, you affirm that you are deserving of a life free from addiction, a life filled with purpose and peace.
5 Affirmations for Day 12
"I am worthy of love, respect, and kindness, both from myself and others."
"I honor my values and live in alignment with my truest self."
"I release any need for validation from others, knowing my worth is within me."
"Each day, I affirm my worth by making choices that support my well-being."
Gratitude Meditation: Recognizing and Embracing Your Worth
Begin by Grounding Yourself: Sit comfortably, close your eyes, and take a few deep breaths. Inhale deeply, and as you exhale, release any doubts or self-judgment, allowing yourself to be fully present in this moment.

Reflect on Your Inherent Worth: Bring to mind the idea that, simply by being you, you are worthy of love, respect, and happiness. Think about the qualities that make you unique - your kindness, your resilience, your capacity for growth. Feel gratitude for these aspects of yourself, recognizing that they contribute to your inherent worth.

Reflect on Three Things You're Grateful For:

First, express gratitude for the unique strengths and qualities that make you who you are, acknowledging that these qualities add value to the world.

Second, thank yourself for choosing to embark on this journey of recovery, as it reflects your belief in your own worth and potential.

Third, appreciate the self-compassion you are cultivating, recognizing that every act of kindness toward yourself affirms your worth.

Visualize Self-Worth as a Golden Light: Imagine a warm, golden light glowing at the center of your chest. This light represents your self-worth - an inherent part of who you are. With each breath, let this light expand, filling your entire body, reminding you that you are enough, just as you are. Feel gratitude for this sense of worth, allowing it to settle within you.

End with a Breath of Affirmation: Take a final deep breath, feeling a deep sense of peace and appreciation for your own worth. Know that your value is not conditional on any action or achievement; it simply exists within you. When you're ready, gently open your eyes, carrying this awareness of your self-worth into the day.

Reflection for Today

In your journal or during a quiet moment, consider these prompts:

What are three qualities I admire in myself?

How does it feel to affirm my worth, independent of external validation?

What choices can I make today that reflect my self-worth and respect for myself?

Today, remember that your worth is not something you need to earn - it's a fundamental part of who you are. By embracing and affirming this truth, you lay a foundation of self-respect and strength that supports you on your journey. You deserve a life that reflects your values, passions, and potential. Embrace this truth, and let it guide you forward.

Chapter 13

Day 13: Finding Strength in Vulnerability
Stoic Quote of the Day
"If you want to improve, be content to be thought foolish and stupid."
- Epictetus
Reflection: Epictetus reminds us that growth often requires stepping outside our comfort zones and risking vulnerability. In recovery, vulnerability can be intimidating - it means confronting fears, expressing needs, and allowing others to see parts of yourself that may feel raw or unpolished. Yet, true strength lies in embracing vulnerability, as it allows you to grow, connect, and build resilience. Today, focus on finding strength in your vulnerability, knowing that it is an integral part of your journey to freedom and healing.
5 Affirmations for Day 13
"I am strong enough to be vulnerable, knowing that growth requires honesty."
"I embrace my emotions fully, allowing myself to experience and express them."
"My vulnerability is a source of connection and authenticity."
"I trust myself to handle my emotions with compassion and understanding."
"Each time I allow myself to be vulnerable, I grow stronger and more authentic."
Gratitude Meditation: Embracing Vulnerability as a Strength
Begin with Gentle Breathing: Sit comfortably, close your eyes, and take a few deep breaths. With each inhale, draw in calm and acceptance; with each exhale, release any fear or hesitation, allowing yourself to settle into a place of openness.

Acknowledge a Moment of Vulnerability: Reflect on a recent moment when you allowed yourself to be vulnerable, whether by sharing a difficult emotion, asking for help, or facing a challenging truth. Recognize the courage it took to embrace this vulnerability and give yourself credit for showing up authentically.

Reflect on Three Things You're Grateful For:

First, express gratitude for your courage to be vulnerable, understanding that this openness is a testament to your strength.

Second, thank yourself for the self-compassion you are developing, knowing that each act of kindness toward yourself is a step toward healing.

Third, appreciate the connections and insights that vulnerability allows, recognizing that by being open, you create space for deeper understanding and connection with others.

Visualize Vulnerability as a Gentle Light Within: Imagine a gentle light at the center of your chest, representing your courage to be vulnerable. See this light radiate warmth and acceptance, filling your body with a sense of peace. Know that this light is always within you, a source of strength that grows brighter each time you embrace your authentic self.

End with a Breath of Acceptance: Take a final deep breath, feeling gratitude for the strength and growth that vulnerability brings. When you're ready, open your eyes gently, carrying a sense of peace and courage with you as you continue your day.

Reflection for Today

In your journal or during a quiet moment, reflect on these prompts:

What does vulnerability mean to me, and how does it feel to embrace it?

How can I remind myself that vulnerability is a form of strength?

In what areas of my life can I be more open and honest with myself and others?

Today, remember that vulnerability is not a weakness - it is a powerful form of strength. By allowing yourself to be open, you create space for growth, healing, and connection. Embrace this courage within, knowing that each step into vulnerability brings you closer to inner freedom and authentic self-acceptance.

Chapter 14

Day 14: Cultivating Inner Peace

Stoic Quote of the Day

"He who lives in harmony with himself lives in harmony with the universe."

- Marcus Aurelius

Reflection: Marcus Aurelius speaks to the power of inner peace, suggesting that by finding balance within ourselves, we can create a sense of harmony with the world around us. In recovery, cultivating inner peace means learning to accept ourselves fully, letting go of inner conflict, and finding calm amid life's challenges. Today, focus on practices that bring you closer to a state of inner tranquility. Embrace stillness, acceptance, and the understanding that peace begins within.

5 Affirmations for Day 14

"I am at peace with myself, accepting all aspects of who I am."

"I release the need for control, trusting that I am capable of facing whatever comes my way."

"I choose to cultivate calm and balance in my thoughts and actions."

"I find peace within myself, allowing me to face life with clarity and strength."

"Each moment of stillness I embrace brings me closer to a life of harmony and freedom."

Gratitude Meditation: Embracing Inner Peace

Settle into Stillness: Find a comfortable position and close your eyes. Take a few deep breaths, inhaling slowly and exhaling gently. With each exhale, imagine releasing any tension, stress, or restlessness, allowing yourself to become fully present and calm.

Reflect on Moments of Peace: Think about a recent moment, however small, when you felt calm and at ease. It could have been during a quiet morning, a walk in nature, or a few seconds of stillness. Allow yourself to reconnect with this feeling, appreciating the sense of peace it brought.

Reflect on Three Things You're Grateful For:

First, express gratitude for your capacity to find peace within yourself, recognizing that this calm is always available to you, even in challenging times.

Second, thank yourself for the steps you've taken toward creating a balanced life, as each act of self-care and mindfulness contributes to your inner harmony.

Third, appreciate the quiet moments and small joys that bring tranquility to your day, reminding you that peace is often found in simplicity.

Visualize Inner Peace as a Still Lake: Picture a calm, still lake within you, reflecting the sky above. Imagine that any thoughts, worries, or anxieties are like ripples on the surface, gradually fading until the lake is smooth and undisturbed. Know that, like this lake, you have the power to return to a state of calm whenever you choose.

End with a Breath of Peace: Take a final deep breath, feeling a profound sense of inner peace and gratitude for your journey. When you're ready, open your eyes, carrying this feeling of tranquility with you throughout your day.

Reflection for Today

In your journal or during a quiet moment, reflect on these prompts:

What practices or activities help me find inner peace?

How can I cultivate more moments of calm and stillness in my daily life?

What does it feel like to embrace peace within myself, regardless of external circumstances?

Today, remember that true peace comes from within. By finding harmony with yourself, you are creating a foundation of resilience, clarity, and strength. Embrace this calmness, knowing that each peaceful moment brings you closer to a life filled with balance, purpose, and freedom.

Chapter 15

Day 15: Developing a Vision for the Future
Stoic Quote of the Day
"Begin at once to live, and count each separate day as a separate life."
- Seneca
Reflection: Seneca reminds us to approach each day as a new opportunity, as if it were a life unto itself. In recovery, it's natural to look forward to the future with both hope and caution. Developing a vision for the life you want to live can inspire you, guiding your choices with purpose. Today, focus on envisioning the future you want to create - one that reflects your values, strengths, and dreams. Allow yourself to imagine a life built on the foundation of freedom, peace, and fulfillment, and recognize that each day, each choice, brings you closer to it.

5 Affirmations for Day 15
"I am worthy of a life that reflects my dreams, values, and strengths."
"I have the power to create a future that aligns with my true self."
"Each step I take today is building the foundation of my dreams."
"I trust myself to envision and work toward a fulfilling, joyful life."
"My life is a work in progress, and each day brings me closer to the person I want to become."

Gratitude Meditation: Envisioning Your Future with Purpose
Find a Comfortable Space: Sit in a quiet place, close your eyes, and take three deep, slow breaths. As you inhale, imagine drawing in hope and purpose; as you exhale, release any doubts or fears about the future, letting yourself relax fully.
Picture Your Ideal Life: Begin to visualize the life you wish to create - one where you feel free, fulfilled, and at peace. Imagine what this

future looks like, the kinds of experiences and relationships you have, and the sense of purpose that guides you. Let this vision fill you with inspiration and hope.

Reflect on Three Things You're Grateful For:

First, express gratitude for your dreams and goals, acknowledging that they give your life direction and meaning.

Second, thank yourself for the commitment you've shown in your journey of growth and recovery, recognizing that each step you take is part of building this future.

Third, appreciate the progress you've already made, knowing that every small victory is a building block for the life you envision.

Visualize Your Vision as a Guiding Star: Imagine your vision for the future as a bright star on the horizon, always shining and guiding you forward. Know that, even if the journey has twists and turns, this vision is there to inspire and motivate you. Feel gratitude for this sense of purpose, as it gives you direction and courage.

End with a Breath of Inspiration: Take a final deep breath, feeling gratitude for your journey and the life you are creating. When you're ready, gently open your eyes, carrying a sense of hope and purpose with you as you move through your day.

Reflection for Today

In your journal or during a quiet moment, reflect on these prompts:

What does my ideal future look like, and what values are most important in it?

How can I begin to bring elements of this vision into my daily life, even in small ways?

What steps can I take today to move closer to the life I want to create?

Today, remember that your future is shaped by each choice, action, and intention. By developing a clear vision, you're creating a roadmap that will guide and inspire you. Embrace the life you're building and know that every day brings you closer to your dreams.

Chapter 16

Day 16: Embracing Change as Growth
Stoic Quote of the Day
"The universe is change; our life is what our thoughts make it."
- Marcus Aurelius
Reflection: Marcus Aurelius reminds us that change is the natural order of life, and that our perspective shapes our experience of it. In recovery, embracing change is essential for growth and transformation. Instead of fearing change, see it as an opportunity - a chance to evolve into a version of yourself that reflects your deepest values and dreams. Today, focus on welcoming change as a pathway to growth, knowing that each shift, no matter how small, brings you closer to a life of freedom and authenticity.
5 Affirmations for Day 16
"I welcome change as a powerful force for growth in my life."
"I am capable of adapting to new circumstances with resilience and grace."
"Each change I embrace brings me closer to my true self and my highest potential."
"I release resistance to change, knowing it is a natural part of my journey."
Accepting change with an Open Heart
Begin with Centered Breathing: Sit comfortably, close your eyes, and take three deep breaths, inhaling slowly and exhaling fully. With each exhale, release any fear or resistance, allowing yourself to be fully present and open to change.
Reflect on Recent Changes: Think about recent changes in your life, big or small. Recognize that each of these changes has been part of your

journey, guiding you toward growth, self-understanding, and healing. Allow yourself to feel grateful for the lessons these changes have brought.

Reflect on Three Things You're Grateful For:

First, express gratitude for your ability to adapt and grow through each change, knowing that resilience is one of your strengths.

Second, thank yourself for the courage to embrace the unknown, recognizing that by welcoming change, you open yourself to new possibilities.

Third, appreciate the growth and wisdom you have gained from each transition, understanding that each change brings you closer to your authentic self.

Visualize Change as a Gentle Breeze: Imagine change as a gentle breeze flowing through your life, bringing in new experiences, perspectives, and opportunities. Picture this breeze sweeping away anything that no longer serves you, making room for growth and freedom. Feel gratitude for the fresh energy that change brings.

End with a Breath of Openness: Take a final deep breath, filling yourself with a sense of openness and gratitude for the journey you're on. When you're ready, gently open your eyes, carrying a sense of calm and acceptance for any changes that may come.

Reflection for Today

In your journal or during a quiet moment, reflect on these prompts:

What recent changes in my life have contributed to my growth?

How can I remind myself to view change as a positive force, even when it feels uncomfortable?

What areas of my life would benefit from embracing change with an open heart?

Today, remember that change is not something to fear - it is an opportunity to become more aligned with who you truly are. By welcoming each new experience as a chance to learn and grow, you are creating a life filled with resilience, strength, and authenticity. Embrace change as a partner on your journey to freedom and fulfillment.

Chapter 17

Day 17: Cultivating Gratitude in Everyday Moments

Stoic Quote of the Day

"He is a wise man who does not grieve for the things which he has not, but rejoices for those which he has."

- Epictetus

Reflection: Epictetus teaches us the power of gratitude, encouraging us to focus on what we have rather than what we lack. In recovery, cultivating gratitude can help shift our mindset from scarcity to abundance, fostering appreciation for the present moment and the small steps we take each day. Today, focus on finding gratitude in everyday moments, recognizing that even the simplest things can bring joy and fulfillment. This practice can serve as a powerful anchor, grounding you in positivity and hope.

5 Affirmations for Day 17

"I am grateful for the progress I have made, no matter how small."

"I choose to focus on the abundance in my life, appreciating each moment fully."

"Gratitude opens my heart and mind to joy, peace, and resilience."

"I am thankful for the journey I am on and the growth it brings me."

"Every day is filled with small blessings, and I am grateful for each one."

Gratitude Meditation: Finding Joy in Small Moments

Start with a Deep Breath: Sit comfortably and close your eyes. Take three slow, deep breaths, inhaling peace and exhaling any tension or negativity. Allow yourself to settle into the present moment, feeling calm and open.

Reflect on Simple Pleasures: Think about small, simple pleasures in your day-to-day life that bring you comfort or joy. This could be the warmth of a morning coffee, a quiet moment of stillness, or the support of a loved one. Recognize that these moments are gifts, and let yourself feel gratitude for each one.

Reflect on Three Things You're Grateful For:

First, express gratitude for the people in your life who bring love, support, or inspiration. Recognize the gift of connection and companionship.

Second, thank yourself for the journey you're on and the steps you're taking each day to build a better life. Appreciate the effort and courage you bring to this path.

Third, acknowledge the present moment, appreciating the opportunity to be here, now, focused on your healing and growth.

Visualize Gratitude as a Warm Light Spreading Through You: Imagine a warm, golden light beginning in your heart, representing gratitude. With each breath, see this light expanding, filling your chest, your entire body, and finally radiating outward, creating a feeling of warmth, peace, and appreciation for life. Know that this gratitude is always within you, ready to be nurtured.

End with a Breath of Appreciation: Take one last deep breath, feeling gratitude for this moment, this journey, and the abundance in your life. When you're ready, open your eyes, carrying a sense of appreciation and joy with you throughout the day.

Reflection for Today

In your journal or during a quiet moment, reflect on these prompts:

What small things in my life am I grateful for today?

How does focusing on gratitude change my perspective on challenges or setbacks?

What can I do each day to cultivate more moments of gratitude and mindfulness?

Today, remember that gratitude is a powerful tool for shifting perspective and finding joy in the present. By appreciating the small blessings in your life, you create a foundation of positivity, resilience, and peace. Embrace this practice of gratitude as a daily ritual, allowing it to deepen your journey and bring greater fulfillment to each moment.

Chapter 18

Day 18: Embracing Self-Reflection and Honesty
Stoic Quote of the Day
"The first and greatest victory is to conquer yourself."
- Plato
Reflection: Plato reminds us that true victory lies in self-mastery, a journey that requires honesty, courage, and reflection. Recovery is a time for self-discovery, to look inward and understand ourselves on a deeper level. Today, focus on practicing self-reflection with honesty and compassion. Embrace your journey, your strengths, and the areas where you can grow. Let this be a day for inner clarity, where you acknowledge your progress and approach your imperfections with acceptance.
5 Affirmations for Day 18
"I have the courage to be honest with myself, knowing that truth leads to growth."
NLP Focus: Encourages self-honesty and frames it as an act of courage, creating a safe space for self-reflection.
"I am committed to self-discovery, learning from both my strengths and my challenges."
NLP Focus: Promotes a growth mindset, embracing all aspects of the self as opportunities for learning.
"I accept myself fully, with both my strengths and areas for growth."
NLP Focus: Builds self-acceptance, reducing judgment and fostering compassion.
"I am constantly evolving, and I honor each step of my journey."
NLP Focus: Affirms progress as a process, encouraging patience and appreciation for the journey.
"Through self-reflection, I gain clarity, wisdom, and peace."

NLP Focus: Connects self-reflection with inner clarity and growth, reinforcing its value.

Gratitude Meditation: Honoring Truth and Self-Reflection

Begin by Calming the Mind: Sit comfortably, close your eyes, and take three deep breaths, slowly inhaling through the nose and exhaling through the mouth. Allow each exhale to release any judgment or self-criticism, creating a space of calm and acceptance.

Reflect on Your Journey of Growth: Think about the progress you've made on this journey. Acknowledge the steps you've taken, no matter how small, and the courage it took to be here. Let yourself feel gratitude for your own honesty and commitment to growth, recognizing that self-reflection is an essential part of your path.

Reflect on Three Things You're Grateful For:

First, express gratitude for your ability to be honest with yourself, knowing that this honesty is a powerful tool for transformation.

Second, thank yourself for the courage to face both your strengths and areas for growth, understanding that self-awareness brings you closer to freedom.

Third, appreciate the wisdom gained from self-reflection, recognizing that each insight brings you closer to a life aligned with your true self.

Visualize Self-Reflection as a Gentle Mirror: Picture a mirror in front of you, clear and kind, reflecting your true self without judgment. Imagine looking into this mirror with compassion, seeing both your strengths and your imperfections. Know that each reflection is a step toward deeper self-understanding, and let yourself feel gratitude for this moment of connection with your authentic self.

End with a Breath of Clarity: Take a final deep breath, feeling a sense of gratitude and clarity. Know that by practicing self-reflection and honesty, you are growing and evolving each day. When you're ready, open your eyes, carrying this sense of peace and clarity with you into the day.

Reflection for Today

In your journal or during a quiet moment, reflect on these prompts:
What have I learned about myself on this journey so far?
How can I continue to practice honesty with myself, especially in challenging moments?
What are some areas in my life where I want to grow, and how can I approach them with compassion?
Today, remember that self-reflection is not about judgment but about understanding. By looking within with honesty and compassion, you empower yourself to grow, evolve, and live authentically. Embrace this practice as a path to deeper self-awareness, knowing that each moment of honesty is a step closer to freedom and inner peace.

Chapter 19

Day 19: Building Resilience Through Acceptance
Stoic Quote of the Day
"The impediment to action advances action. What stands in the way becomes the way."
- Marcus Aurelius
Reflection: Marcus Aurelius teaches us that obstacles can become our teachers, guiding us toward resilience and strength. In recovery, challenges often feel like setbacks, but with acceptance, they can serve as stepping stones for growth. Today, focus on embracing acceptance - not as a passive act but as a powerful choice that allows you to respond rather than react. By accepting challenges, you can transform them into opportunities to grow stronger and more resilient.
5 Affirmations for Day 19
"I embrace each challenge as an opportunity to grow and strengthen my resilience."
"I accept what I cannot control and focus on what I can change."
"I trust myself to handle any obstacle with patience, strength, and grace."
"Every setback I face brings me closer to my inner strength."
"I choose to respond to challenges with courage and calm."
Gratitude Meditation: Embracing Acceptance as a Path to Strength
Start with Deep, Centering Breaths: Sit comfortably, close your eyes, and take three deep breaths, inhaling calm and exhaling resistance. Let each breath guide you toward a place of peace and acceptance.
Acknowledge Current Challenges: Bring to mind a recent challenge or obstacle you've faced. Instead of resisting or wishing it away, allow yourself to accept it as part of your journey. Recognize that this

challenge is an opportunity to strengthen your resilience, teaching you something valuable about yourself.

Reflect on Three Things You're Grateful For:

First, express gratitude for your strength and resilience, acknowledging that you have the power to face any challenge that comes your way.

Second, thank yourself for your willingness to embrace acceptance, understanding that acceptance is a path to peace and clarity.

Third, appreciate the growth that challenges bring, recognizing that each experience, even difficult ones, helps you become the person you are meant to be.

Visualize Acceptance as a Gentle River: Imagine yourself standing beside a gentle river, watching it flow naturally around rocks and obstacles. Visualize your own journey like this river, embracing each bend and change as a part of the path. Let yourself feel gratitude for this flow, understanding that acceptance allows you to navigate life's twists and turns with ease and resilience.

End with a Breath of Strength: Take a final deep breath, feeling a sense of gratitude and strength. Know that by embracing acceptance, you are building resilience and creating a foundation of inner peace. When you're ready, gently open your eyes, carrying this sense of calm and courage with you into the day.

Reflection for Today

In your journal or during a quiet moment, reflect on these prompts:

What challenges have I faced recently, and what have they taught me?

How can I practice acceptance in moments of difficulty, allowing myself to respond rather than react?

In what ways can I build resilience through acceptance, embracing each experience as part of my growth?

Today, remember that acceptance is not about giving up but about letting go of resistance. By embracing each experience with openness, you transform challenges into stepping stones, building resilience, strength, and a sense of peace. Trust in your ability to navigate whatever comes your way, knowing that each moment of acceptance brings you closer to inner freedom and fulfillment.

Chapter 20

Day 20: Practicing Kindness Toward Yourself
Stoic Quote of the Day
"Remember, you have been criticizing yourself for years, and it hasn't worked. Try approving of yourself and see what happens."
- Louise Hay
Reflection: Kindness toward ourselves is often overlooked but deeply transformative. In recovery, self-compassion plays a critical role in healing and rebuilding. Instead of criticizing yourself for past mistakes, try treating yourself with kindness, understanding, and patience. Today, focus on extending the same gentleness to yourself that you would offer to someone you love. Kindness fosters resilience, creates inner peace, and strengthens your commitment to growth.
5 Affirmations for Day 20
"I choose to treat myself with kindness, understanding that I am worthy of compassion."
"I forgive myself for past mistakes and focus on the positive changes I am making."
"I honor my journey, knowing that healing is a process that requires patience."
"I am gentle with myself in moments of struggle, offering love instead of judgment."
"Today, I choose to support myself with kindness and encouragement."
Gratitude Meditation: Cultivating Self-Kindness
Begin with a Gentle Breath: Sit comfortably, close your eyes, and take a few deep breaths. With each exhale, release any tension, self-judgment, or criticism. Allow yourself to settle into a state of calm, ready to embrace kindness toward yourself.

Acknowledge Your Efforts and Growth: Reflect on the effort and commitment you've shown in your journey. Recognize that each step you've taken, no matter how small, is a testament to your strength and determination. Allow yourself to feel gratitude for your resilience, honoring the progress you've made with compassion.

Reflect on Three Things You're Grateful For:

First, express gratitude for your ability to be kind to yourself, understanding that self-compassion is an essential part of healing and growth.

Second, thank yourself for the courage it takes to embrace this journey, recognizing that self-kindness is a powerful tool for transformation.

Third, appreciate the progress you've made, no matter how gradual, as each step forward brings you closer to inner peace and freedom.

Visualize Kindness as a Warm Embrace: Imagine a soft, warm light surrounding you, like a gentle embrace. This light represents kindness and compassion. With each breath, let this warmth fill you, soothing any harsh self-criticism and leaving only acceptance and peace. Know that this kindness is always available to you, ready to support you in moments of struggle.

End with a Breath of Compassion: Take a final deep breath, feeling a sense of peace and gratitude for the kindness you are cultivating toward yourself. When you're ready, gently open your eyes, carrying this sense of warmth and compassion with you throughout the day.

Reflection for Today

In your journal or during a quiet moment, reflect on these prompts:

What are some ways I can be kinder to myself during moments of challenge?

How does it feel to treat myself with the same kindness I offer to others?

What positive changes might come from embracing self-compassion more fully in my life?

Today, remember that kindness toward yourself is a powerful act of healing. By choosing to treat yourself with gentleness and understanding, you are building a foundation of self-compassion that will support you in every stage of your journey. Embrace this kindness as a daily practice, knowing that each moment of self-compassion brings you closer to the life you want to live.

Chapter 21

Day 21: Letting Go of Perfectionism
Stoic Quote of the Day
"Don't aim at perfection. Aim at being authentic."
- Thich Nhat Hanh
Reflection: In a world that often promotes perfection, it's easy to fall into the trap of thinking that only perfection is enough. However, striving for perfection can lead to disappointment, frustration, and self-judgment. Today, focus on letting go of the need to be perfect and instead embrace authenticity and progress. Recovery, like life, is a journey of growth, not flawless execution. Allow yourself the freedom to be imperfect, to make mistakes, and to learn along the way.
5 Affirmations for Day 21
"I release the need for perfection and embrace the beauty of progress."
NLP Focus: Encourages letting go of unrealistic standards and reframing growth as success.
"I am enough as I am, and I am worthy of compassion and acceptance."
"I learn from my mistakes, knowing they are part of my journey."
"I choose authenticity over perfection, allowing myself to be real and honest."
"Each day, I grow stronger by embracing both my strengths and imperfections."
Gratitude Meditation: Embracing Imperfection
Start with a Deep Breath of Release: Sit comfortably, close your eyes, and take three slow, deep breaths. As you exhale, release any pressure or expectations of perfection. Allow yourself to be fully present, knowing that you are enough exactly as you are.

Acknowledge Your Unique Journey: Reflect on the uniqueness of your journey and the progress you have made, imperfections and all. Recognize that every mistake and every success has contributed to your growth. Allow yourself to feel gratitude for the journey, not as a quest for perfection but as a path toward wholeness and authenticity.

Reflect on Three Things You're Grateful For:

First, express gratitude for the lessons that imperfections have taught you, recognizing that growth often comes from missteps and setbacks.

Second, thank yourself for embracing this journey with authenticity, knowing that real progress comes from being true to yourself.

Third, appreciate the small steps you take each day, understanding that progress is more valuable than perfection.

Visualize Acceptance as a Gentle Flowing River: Imagine yourself standing beside a river that flows gently and naturally, unconcerned with perfection or expectation. Picture yourself letting go of any need for perfection, allowing your journey to flow with ease, taking its natural path. Feel gratitude for this release, trusting that each step, imperfect as it may be, is part of a larger, beautiful journey.

End with a Breath of Freedom: Take a final deep breath, feeling a sense of peace and freedom from perfectionism. When you're ready, gently open your eyes, carrying a sense of authenticity and self-acceptance with you into the day.

Reflection for Today

In your journal or during a quiet moment, reflect on these prompts:

What areas of my life do I tend to hold unrealistic expectations of perfection?

How can I remind myself to value authenticity and progress over perfection?

What benefits can come from embracing my imperfections as part of my unique journey?

Today, remember that letting go of perfectionism opens the door to greater joy, authenticity, and peace. By allowing yourself to be real, to make mistakes, and to continue growing, you free yourself to live fully and embrace your journey without judgment. Each step, no matter how imperfect, brings you closer to the life you want to create.

Chapter 22

Day 22: Practicing Mindfulness in the Present Moment
Stoic Quote of the Day
"The happiness of your life depends upon the quality of your thoughts."
- Marcus Aurelius
Reflection: Marcus Aurelius reminds us of the power of our thoughts and the importance of living in the present. In recovery, practicing mindfulness allows us to stay connected to the moment rather than getting lost in past regrets or future anxieties. Today, focus on being fully present. Mindfulness isn't about perfection; it's about gently bringing your attention back to now whenever your mind starts to wander. The present is where peace, clarity, and true freedom reside.
5 Affirmations for Day 22
"I am present in this moment, allowing myself to experience it fully."
"I release the past and future, focusing on what I can appreciate right now."
"Each mindful breath I take grounds me in calm and clarity."
"I am open to the beauty of this moment, however simple or ordinary."
"Today, I choose to be fully engaged in my life, moment by moment."
Gratitude Meditation: Embracing the Present
Settle into the Moment: Sit comfortably, close your eyes, and take three slow, deep breaths, inhaling through the nose and exhaling through the mouth. As you breathe, let go of any distractions, worries, or expectations. Allow yourself to be fully here, right now.
Focus on Your Senses: Gently bring awareness to your senses - the feeling of your body against the chair, the sounds around you, the temperature of the air. Take a moment to be fully immersed in these sensations without judgment, simply noticing what is present.

Reflect on Three Things You're Grateful For Right Now:
First, express gratitude for the ability to be present, acknowledging that mindfulness brings you peace and clarity.
Second, thank yourself for taking the time to nurture your mind and spirit, recognizing the power of presence in your healing journey.
Third, appreciate the small details of this moment, whether it's the comfort of your seat, the stillness around you, or the feeling of your breath.
Visualize Your Thoughts as Passing Clouds: Imagine any thoughts or worries that arise as clouds drifting across a clear sky. Notice them, but allow them to pass by without attachment. Gently bring your focus back to your breath, feeling gratitude for this moment of peace and presence.
End with a Breath of Presence: Take a final deep breath, feeling grounded, calm, and connected to the here and now. When you're ready, open your eyes gently, carrying this sense of presence and mindfulness with you as you move through the day.

Reflection for Today

In your journal or during a quiet moment, reflect on these prompts:
How does it feel to focus fully on the present moment?
What benefits do I notice when I practice mindfulness in my daily life?
What are some small ways I can incorporate mindfulness into my routine, even during busy moments?
Today, remember that mindfulness is a gift you can give to yourself each day. By being fully present, you free yourself from the weight of the past and the worries of the future. Embrace each moment, knowing that true peace is found in the here and now. Allow this practice of mindfulness to ground you, inspire you, and bring you closer to a life filled with clarity and contentment.

Chapter 23

Day 23: Embracing the Power of Forgiveness
Stoic Quote of the Day
"To forgive is to set a prisoner free and discover that the prisoner was you."
- Lewis B. Smedes
Reflection: Forgiveness is a powerful act of liberation, allowing us to release resentment and heal. In recovery, forgiveness isn't just about others; it's about freeing yourself from past mistakes and regrets. Today, focus on practicing forgiveness toward yourself and others, recognizing that letting go of resentment opens space for peace and freedom. Forgiveness doesn't mean forgetting; it means no longer allowing past hurts to dictate your present or future.
5 Affirmations for Day 23
"I release resentment and embrace the peace that forgiveness brings."
"I forgive myself for past mistakes, understanding that they are part of my growth."
"I choose to move forward with a heart free from grudges or anger."
"Forgiveness is my gift to myself, allowing me to heal and grow."
"Each act of forgiveness brings me closer to inner peace and freedom."
Gratitude Meditation: Cultivating a Forgiving Heart
Settle into a Peaceful Space: Sit comfortably, close your eyes, and take three deep breaths. With each exhale, imagine releasing tension or resentment, creating space in your heart for forgiveness and peace.
Reflect on an Area of Your Life Where Forgiveness is Needed: Bring to mind a situation, either involving yourself or someone else, where forgiveness is needed. Allow yourself to approach this memory with

compassion and a willingness to let go. Acknowledge the pain, but remind yourself that forgiveness is about freeing yourself from its hold.

Reflect on Three Things You're Grateful For:

First, express gratitude for your capacity to forgive, recognizing that this ability brings you closer to inner peace.

Second, thank yourself for the courage to let go of past hurts, appreciating the strength it takes to choose forgiveness over resentment.

Third, appreciate the lightness and freedom that forgiveness brings, allowing you to move forward with a clear heart.

Visualize Forgiveness as a Soothing Light: Imagine a warm, soothing light surrounding your heart, softening any pain or resentment. Feel this light as a source of peace, gradually filling you with warmth and compassion. As it expands, imagine it gently releasing any lingering anger or hurt, leaving you with a sense of calm and freedom.

End with a Breath of Release: Take a final deep breath, letting go of any residual tension, knowing that forgiveness is an act of self-love and liberation. When you're ready, open your eyes, carrying a sense of peace and openness with you into your day.

Reflection for Today

In your journal or during a quiet moment, reflect on these prompts:

Who or what do I feel ready to forgive, and how can I begin that process?

How does forgiving myself and others create space for peace in my life?

What benefits can I envision from carrying less resentment and more compassion?

Today, remember that forgiveness is a journey, not a one-time act. By choosing to forgive, you release the weight of the past and allow yourself to live more freely in the present. Embrace the power of forgiveness as a tool for healing, understanding that each step brings you closer to a life filled with peace, growth, and inner harmony.

Chapter 24

Day 24: Embracing Self-Discipline with Compassion
Stoic Quote of the Day
"No man is free who is not master of himself."
- Epictetus
Reflection: Epictetus reminds us that true freedom comes from self-mastery. In recovery, cultivating self-discipline can help you stay committed to your journey while building resilience. However, discipline does not mean harshness; it means setting boundaries with kindness and supporting your growth. Today, focus on practicing self-discipline with compassion, creating habits that strengthen your resolve while being gentle with yourself when challenges arise. By balancing discipline with self-compassion, you nurture a foundation of strength and self-respect.
5 Affirmations for Day 24
"I practice self-discipline with kindness, knowing that each step forward brings me closer to my goals."
"I am capable of making choices that honor my growth and well-being."
"Each act of discipline I embrace is a step toward my true freedom."
"I forgive myself for any setbacks and focus on moving forward with purpose."
"I honor my journey by nurturing habits that align with my values."
Gratitude Meditation: Embracing Self-Discipline as Self-Love
Begin with a Centering Breath: Sit comfortably, close your eyes, and take three slow, deep breaths. With each exhale, release any judgment or harshness, allowing yourself to settle into a state of calm acceptance.
Reflect on Your Commitment to Growth: Acknowledge the dedication you have shown to your recovery journey. Recognize that

self-discipline is a form of self-love, as it reinforces your commitment to living a life that honors your values and goals. Allow yourself to feel gratitude for this commitment.

Reflect on Three Things You're Grateful For:

First, express gratitude for the self-discipline you are developing, recognizing that each moment of commitment strengthens your resolve.

Second, thank yourself for choosing habits that support your well-being, understanding that each positive choice is a step toward freedom.

Third, appreciate the balance you are creating between discipline and self-compassion, knowing that this balance is essential for long-term growth.

Visualize Discipline as a Steady Flame: Picture self-discipline as a steady, warm flame within you, one that grows brighter with each choice you make to honor your journey. Imagine this flame representing your strength, resilience, and commitment to yourself. Feel gratitude for this flame, knowing it is a source of inner power and self-respect.

End with a Breath of Empowerment: Take a final deep breath, feeling a sense of strength and peace in your commitment to yourself. When you're ready, open your eyes, carrying this sense of self-discipline and compassion with you throughout the day.

Reflection for Today

In your journal or during a quiet moment, reflect on these prompts:

How can I practice self-discipline in a way that feels supportive rather than restrictive?

What habits or actions can I commit to today that align with my goals and values?

How can I remind myself to be compassionate with myself if I encounter setbacks?

Today, remember that self-discipline is a powerful tool for personal freedom, but it thrives best when balanced with self-compassion. By honoring your journey with choices that reflect your values and being gentle with yourself when challenges arise, you are creating a strong foundation for lasting growth. Embrace self-discipline as a form of self-love, knowing that each step forward brings you closer to the life you want to live.

Chapter 25

Day 25: Releasing the Need for Control

Stoic Quote of the Day

"You have power over your mind - not outside events. Realize this, and you will find strength."

- Marcus Aurelius

Reflection: Marcus Aurelius reminds us that true strength lies in letting go of what we cannot control and focusing instead on our thoughts, responses, and inner peace. In recovery, it's natural to feel a desire to control outcomes, circumstances, or the actions of others. But peace comes from releasing this need for control and trusting the journey. Today, focus on embracing what you can control - your reactions, your mindset, and your daily choices - and letting go of what lies outside of your influence.

5 Affirmations for Day 25

"I release the need for control and trust in the journey I am on."

"I focus on what I can control - my thoughts, actions, and responses."

"I am free from the stress of controlling everything and embrace peace in the present moment."

"I choose to respond to life with calm and acceptance, knowing that I am enough."

"Today, I release fear and allow myself to flow with life's natural rhythms."

Gratitude Meditation: Embracing Surrender and Trust

Begin with a Deep Breath of Release: Sit comfortably, close your eyes, and take three slow, deep breaths. With each exhale, imagine releasing any tension, control, or need to dictate the outcome. Allow yourself to settle into the present moment.

Reflect on What You Can Control: Bring to mind the things you truly have control over - your mindset, actions, and how you respond to circumstances. Recognize that these are your sources of strength and resilience. Feel gratitude for your ability to influence your own thoughts and choices.

Reflect on Three Things You're Grateful For:

First, express gratitude for the strength within you to adapt to life's changes, knowing that you are capable of handling whatever comes your way.

Second, thank yourself for releasing stress over what lies outside of your control, allowing more peace to enter your life.

Third, appreciate the sense of freedom that comes from letting go of control, embracing the natural flow of your journey.

Visualize Letting Go as a Feather Floating Away: Imagine any worries, fears, or need for control as a feather in your hand. Picture yourself releasing it into the air, watching it float away peacefully. Feel a sense of lightness as you let go, trusting in life's natural rhythm and flow.

End with a Breath of Trust: Take a final deep breath, feeling a sense of calm and gratitude for the freedom of releasing control. When you're ready, gently open your eyes, carrying this peace and acceptance with you into the day.

Reflection for Today

In your journal or during a quiet moment, reflect on these prompts:

What areas of my life am I holding too tightly, and how can I release some control?

How can I remind myself to focus on what I can influence rather than what I cannot?

What benefits might come from letting go and trusting in the journey?

Today, remember that true peace comes from embracing the flow of life rather than trying to control every aspect of it. By focusing on what lies within your control and letting go of the rest, you open yourself to greater freedom, resilience, and calm. Embrace this practice of surrender, knowing that each moment of letting go brings you closer to inner peace.

Chapter 26

Day 26: Nurturing Self-Respect
Stoic Quote of the Day
"Respect yourself, and others will respect you."
- Confucius
Reflection: Confucius reminds us that self-respect is the foundation upon which healthy relationships and positive interactions are built. In recovery, nurturing self-respect involves honoring your boundaries, values, and personal growth. Self-respect encourages you to make choices that reflect your worth and support your well-being. Today, focus on cultivating self-respect through mindful choices, self-care, and standing by your values. By respecting yourself, you strengthen your commitment to a life of integrity and authenticity.
5 Affirmations for Day 26
"I respect myself, my journey, and the progress I am making."
"I honor my boundaries, knowing they are essential to my well-being."
"I am worthy of choices that align with my values and reflect my worth."
"I treat myself with the same kindness and respect that I offer to others."
"Each day, I choose actions that reflect my respect for myself and my journey."
Gratitude Meditation: Cultivating Self-Respect and Inner Dignity
Begin with a Grounding Breath: Sit comfortably, close your eyes, and take three deep breaths. With each exhale, release any self-doubt or negativity. Allow yourself to settle into a space of calm and self-acceptance.
Reflect on Moments of Self-Respect: Think of a recent moment when you honored yourself - by setting a boundary, choosing an action aligned with your values, or treating yourself with kindness. Recognize

that these moments of self-respect strengthen your confidence and self-worth. Allow yourself to feel gratitude for your commitment to honoring yourself.

Reflect on Three Things You're Grateful For:

First, express gratitude for your ability to respect yourself and make choices that support your growth.

Second, thank yourself for the boundaries you set and the standards you hold, knowing that these choices are acts of self-love.

Third, appreciate the sense of dignity that comes from living a life true to your values and beliefs.

Visualize Self-Respect as a Radiant Shield: Picture self-respect as a radiant, protective shield around you. This shield reflects your values, boundaries, and integrity. Imagine it growing stronger with each choice you make that aligns with your true self. Feel gratitude for this shield, knowing it supports and protects you on your journey.

End with a Breath of Dignity: Take a final deep breath, feeling grounded in your self-respect and inner strength. When you're ready, gently open your eyes, carrying a sense of dignity and respect with you throughout the day.

Reflection for Today

In your journal or during a quiet moment, reflect on these prompts:

How do I show respect for myself in my daily choices?

What are some ways I can continue to honor my boundaries and values?

How does nurturing self-respect impact my recovery and overall well-being?

Today, remember that self-respect is both a foundation and a practice. By honoring yourself, you build a life that reflects your true worth and supports your healing. Embrace self-respect as an essential part of your journey, knowing that each respectful choice brings you closer to a life of integrity, peace, and inner strength.

Chapter 27

Day 27: Embracing Gratitude for Your Strengths
Stoic Quote of the Day
"The only wealth which you will keep forever is the wealth you have given away."
- Marcus Aurelius
Reflection: Marcus Aurelius speaks to the lasting value of internal wealth - qualities like kindness, resilience, and strength - that remain with us and can also uplift others. In recovery, embracing gratitude for your strengths reminds you of the inner resources that help you persevere, grow, and support others on similar journeys. Today, focus on recognizing and celebrating your strengths, acknowledging the unique qualities that have carried you through difficult times. By embracing these strengths, you can build confidence and trust in your ability to navigate the road ahead.
5 Affirmations for Day 27
"I am grateful for the strengths that make me resilient and capable."
"I trust my inner strengths to guide me through each day with courage."
"Each of my strengths brings value to my life and the lives of others."
"I celebrate my progress and the qualities that support my growth."
"Today, I honor the unique strengths within me that shape my journey."
Gratitude Meditation: Honoring Your Inner Strengths
Settle into a Comfortable Position: Sit comfortably, close your eyes, and take three deep breaths. With each exhale, let go of any doubt or self-criticism, allowing yourself to fully embrace and honor the strengths within you.
Reflect on the Strengths You Hold: Think of a few qualities that you consider your strengths - whether it's resilience, compassion, patience,

or courage. Recognize that these strengths have been instrumental in your journey and have helped you overcome challenges. Let yourself feel gratitude for each of these unique qualities.

Reflect on Three Things You're Grateful For:
First, express gratitude for the resilience you've shown throughout your journey, recognizing that it has helped you endure and grow.

Second, thank yourself for the kindness and compassion you offer to others and yourself, knowing that these qualities enrich your life and relationships.

Third, appreciate the courage it takes to continue moving forward, acknowledging that courage is a strength that has guided you through difficult times.

Visualize Your Strengths as a Steady Light Within You: Picture each of your strengths as a steady light within your chest, growing brighter with each breath. Imagine this light as a source of guidance, resilience, and warmth, ready to support you whenever needed. Feel gratitude for this light, knowing it represents the unique gifts and qualities that make you who you are.

End with a Breath of Confidence: Take a final deep breath, filling yourself with gratitude for your inner strengths and the journey they've supported. When you're ready, gently open your eyes, carrying a sense of self-respect, confidence, and appreciation with you throughout the day.

Reflection for Today
In your journal or during a quiet moment, reflect on these prompts:
What are three strengths I recognize in myself, and how have they supported my growth?
How can I celebrate and honor my strengths in my daily actions?
How does focusing on my strengths build my confidence and resilience in recovery?
Today, remember that your strengths are not just tools for survival but qualities that make you unique and capable. By embracing and

celebrating these qualities, you are reinforcing your belief in yourself and your ability to continue moving forward. Trust in your strengths, knowing they are a source of support, resilience, and light on your journey to inner freedom.

Chapter 28

Day 28: Fostering a Spirit of Generosity
Stoic Quote of the Day
"The wise man does not lay up his own treasures. The more he gives to others, the more he has for his own."
- Lao Tzu
Reflection: Lao Tzu reminds us that generosity enriches both the giver and the receiver. In recovery, generosity can take many forms - whether it's offering a listening ear, sharing encouragement, or simply showing kindness to others. Today, focus on cultivating a spirit of generosity, knowing that by sharing your strength and compassion, you uplift yourself as well. Acts of generosity, no matter how small, create a sense of connection, purpose, and fulfillment that nurtures both your spirit and the spirits of others.
5 Affirmations for Day 28
"I am grateful for the opportunity to give and connect with others."
"My acts of kindness bring warmth and fulfillment to my heart."
"I have an abundance of love and compassion to share with others."
"Each act of generosity strengthens my spirit and sense of purpose."
"Today, I choose to uplift others, knowing that generosity enriches my life."
Gratitude Meditation: Embracing the Joy of Giving
Begin with a Breath of Openness: Sit comfortably, close your eyes, and take three slow, deep breaths. With each exhale, release any hesitation or worry. Allow yourself to settle into a state of calm openness, ready to give and receive positivity.
Reflect on Acts of Generosity: Think of a time when someone showed you kindness or when you were able to help someone else. Reflect on

how these acts made you feel - whether it was a sense of connection, gratitude, or warmth. Allow yourself to feel gratitude for the ways that generosity has touched your life.

Reflect on Three Things You're Grateful For:
First, express gratitude for the people who have shown you kindness and generosity, recognizing the impact these acts have had on your journey.

Second, thank yourself for the times you have shared your own kindness and support with others, knowing that these actions have enriched your life and theirs.

Third, appreciate the opportunities for connection and compassion that generosity brings, understanding that giving creates a circle of positivity in your life.

Visualize Generosity as a Flowing River: Imagine generosity as a river flowing through you, connecting you to others. This river is endless, abundant, and filled with kindness. As you give, this river grows stronger, creating a sense of joy and fulfillment. Feel gratitude for this river of connection, knowing it enriches you each time you allow it to flow.

End with a Breath of Abundance: Take a final deep breath, feeling a sense of openness and fulfillment. When you're ready, gently open your eyes, carrying a spirit of generosity and connection with you into the day.

Reflection for Today
In your journal or during a quiet moment, reflect on these prompts:
What are some simple ways I can share kindness and generosity with others today?
How does giving to others positively impact my own sense of purpose and fulfillment?
What benefits do I feel when I embrace a spirit of generosity in my daily life?

Today, remember that generosity is not about the size of the gesture but the spirit with which it is given. By choosing to share kindness, compassion, and support, you create a life that is rich in connection and fulfillment. Embrace the joy of giving, knowing that each act of generosity strengthens your spirit and brings you closer to a life of inner peace and harmony.

Chapter 29

Day 29: Celebrating Progress and Small Victories
Stoic Quote of the Day
"Well-being is attained by little and little, and nevertheless is no little thing itself."
- Zeno of Citium
Reflection: Zeno reminds us that true well-being is built gradually, through small, consistent efforts that add up over time. In recovery, it's essential to recognize and celebrate each small victory, no matter how modest it may seem. Today, focus on acknowledging your progress and the small steps that have led you to this moment. Each accomplishment, whether big or small, is a testament to your resilience and dedication to growth. Celebrating these milestones reinforces your motivation and reminds you of how far you've come.
5 Affirmations for Day 29
"I honor each small victory, knowing it brings me closer to my goals."
"Every step forward is a testament to my strength and resilience."
"I am proud of the progress I have made, and I trust myself to keep going."
"I celebrate my journey, knowing that each moment contributes to my growth."
"Today, I choose to recognize my progress and give myself credit for my efforts."
Gratitude Meditation: Honoring Your Journey and Progress
Begin with a Breath of Gratitude: Sit comfortably, close your eyes, and take three deep breaths. With each inhale, breathe in gratitude, and with each exhale, release any self-doubt or criticism. Allow yourself to settle into a state of appreciation for your journey.

Reflect on Milestones and Small Victories: Think of the steps you've taken, the challenges you've overcome, and the progress you've made. Whether these victories are big or small, recognize that each one has been essential to your growth. Allow yourself to feel gratitude for each of these moments, knowing they are a testament to your strength.

Reflect on Three Things You're Grateful For:

First, express gratitude for the resilience that has carried you through difficult times, knowing that this resilience is a part of who you are.

Second, thank yourself for each effort and action you've taken toward your goals, recognizing that each step forward is a sign of your dedication.

Third, appreciate the journey itself, understanding that each moment of progress, reflection, and growth has brought you closer to a fulfilling, free life.

Visualize Your Progress as a Path of Light: Imagine your journey as a path illuminated by each small victory - a glowing, steady trail leading you forward. Picture each accomplishment as a light along this path, showing you how far you've come and guiding you toward your future. Feel gratitude for each light on this path, knowing that it represents your progress and growth.

End with a Breath of Celebration: Take a final deep breath, feeling a sense of pride and joy for your progress. When you're ready, gently open your eyes, carrying this sense of celebration and accomplishment with you throughout the day.

Reflection for Today

In your journal or during a quiet moment, reflect on these prompts:

What are some of the small victories I've achieved that I can celebrate today?

How does recognizing my progress help me stay motivated and positive about my journey?

What can I do to honor and celebrate my progress, even in small ways?

Today, remember that each step forward is meaningful, and every small victory deserves to be celebrated. By recognizing your progress, you reinforce your commitment to growth and build a foundation of resilience and pride. Embrace each milestone as a sign of your strength and dedication, knowing that every step brings you closer to the life you envision.

Chapter 30

Day 30: Reflecting on the Journey and Setting Intentions for the Future

Stoic Quote of the Day

"The journey is what brings us happiness, not the destination."
- Dan Millman

Reflection: As your 30-day journey comes to a close, take a moment to honor the growth, resilience, and self-discovery you've experienced. Recovery is a continuous path, and each day is an opportunity to build upon the strength you've nurtured. Today, focus on reflecting on the lessons you've learned, the progress you've made, and the intentions you wish to set for the future. Know that every step forward is an affirmation of your commitment to inner freedom, peace, and fulfillment.

5 Affirmations for Day 30

"I am grateful for the journey of growth, healing, and self-discovery that I have embraced."

"I carry the lessons of this journey with me, knowing they will guide me forward."

"I trust myself to continue making choices that support my well-being and happiness."

"I am proud of the progress I've made and excited for the growth that lies ahead."

"Today, I set my intentions for the future, confident in my strength and resilience."

Gratitude Meditation: Reflecting on Your Journey and Embracing the Future

Settle into a Place of Calm: Sit comfortably, close your eyes, and take three deep breaths, letting each exhale release any lingering tension or worry. Allow yourself to relax into a space of gratitude, ready to honor the journey you've been on.

Reflect on Your Journey: Think back on the past 30 days, acknowledging the growth, challenges, and victories you've experienced. Recognize the strength, resilience, and dedication that have brought you to this point. Allow yourself to feel gratitude for each moment, knowing that each step has been valuable.

Reflect on Three Things You're Grateful For:

First, express gratitude for the commitment you've shown to your healing and well-being, recognizing that this dedication is a powerful act of self-love.

Second, thank yourself for the resilience you've developed, knowing that this inner strength will support you in the future.

Third, appreciate the insights and self-awareness you've gained, understanding that these lessons will continue to guide you forward.

Visualize Your Future as a Path of Light: Imagine a bright, open path in front of you, symbolizing the future. Picture yourself walking along this path, carrying with you all the strength, wisdom, and self-love you've cultivated. Feel gratitude for this journey and trust in the path ahead, knowing you are capable of facing anything that comes your way.

End with a Breath of Intention: Take a final deep breath, setting a personal intention for your future. Whether it's continued healing, self-compassion, or resilience, allow this intention to fill you with a sense of purpose and peace. When you're ready, gently open your eyes, carrying a sense of gratitude, strength, and optimism with you.

Reflection for Today

In your journal or during a quiet moment, reflect on these prompts:

What have been the most valuable lessons I've learned during this journey?

How can I carry the strengths and insights I've gained into my future?

What intentions do I want to set for myself as I move forward?

Today, honor yourself for the commitment, courage, and dedication you've shown over these 30 days. This journey has been one of profound growth, healing, and self-discovery. As you step forward, remember that each day is an opportunity to build on this foundation. Set intentions that reflect your values and dreams, and know that you are fully capable of creating a life filled with inner freedom, peace, and purpose. Embrace the path ahead with confidence and gratitude, knowing that you are strong, resilient, and ready for whatever comes next.

Epilogue

Final Reflections: Embracing the Journey Ahead
Congratulations on completing this 30-day journey! Taking this time for self-reflection, healing, and growth is a profound accomplishment, a testament to your strength and commitment to inner freedom. Each day, you have cultivated resilience, embraced self-compassion, and deepened your understanding of yourself. You've honored your progress, celebrated small victories, and built a foundation for a future aligned with your true self.

Remember that recovery, growth, and well-being are lifelong journeys. The lessons you've gathered over these 30 days will continue to guide you, and each day is an opportunity to apply what you've learned. The practices of mindfulness, forgiveness, self-discipline, and gratitude are powerful tools you can carry forward. Whenever challenges arise, know that the resilience and strength you have cultivated are always within you.

Continuing the Journey
As you move forward, embrace each new day as an opportunity to deepen your connection with yourself, to show kindness, and to continue building a life that reflects your values and dreams. Whether you revisit these daily practices or develop new ones, remember that the journey is not about perfection but about progress, presence, and peace.

Final Affirmation
"I am grateful for this journey of growth and healing. I carry my strength, resilience, and compassion forward, confident in my ability to create a life of peace, purpose, and freedom."

Your path is one of courage and transformation. Embrace it with gratitude, trust in your inner strength, and celebrate the person you are becoming.

Also by Kenneth Thomas

The Convergence of Minds series
The Digital Agora: A Philosophical Epic of AI and Humanity
Beyond the Agora: Fractured Realms

The Veil of Shadows Series
Shattered Dominion
The Fractured Path

Standalone
A Tail of Darkness To Light
The Mirror Within
Echoes of Ink and Heart
Purpose Over Power: The Visionary Path of Servant Leadership
The Questions That Shape Us: Finding Life's Wisdom-The Power of Inquiry
Where the Shadows Settle
30 Days to Inner Freedom: A Mindful Journey in Addiction Recovery

About the Author

Kenneth Thomas is the founder and CEO of Visionary Tide Media, a pioneering company dedicated to creating transformative media and advanced AI solutions. With over two decades of personal experience in addiction recovery, Kenneth brings a unique perspective to his work, blending deep personal insights with professional expertise. His writing covers a broad spectrum, including AI innovation, personal growth, spirituality, and societal improvement, all aimed at making a meaningful impact. Kenneth's commitment to truth, ethics, and the betterment of humanity is evident in his diverse projects, which include published works, media content, and AI-driven initiatives. Through Visionary Tide Media, he aspires to inspire, educate, and elevate his audience, fostering a world enriched by genuine understanding and compassion.